Sunny Hale

I want to be a

CHAMPION

Sunny Hale

www.sunnyhalepolo.com

I want to be a

CHAMPION

A Champion's letter to kids with a dream

SUNNY HALE

DEDICATION

    I dedicate this book to every kid who has a dream buried within them. This book is for you. Let this be your guide and your reassurance that it is possible. Your dream is your personal gift. It is up to you to open the gift and bring it to life. Do it, mean it and enjoy the journey.

Good luck and don't give up.

Sunny

CONTENTS

CHAPTER ONE

IN THE BEGINNING…

In the beginning of every Champion's story, there is the actual "first step that they took towards their dream". That first step is the most important one to take, because it holds the most power and sometimes it holds pure magic in what will unfold right before your eyes. That first step in the beginning, is also the hardest one you will take on the entire journey.

That first step, is to truly believe in the dream that was planted in you. It was planted there for a reason. I am here to tell you from my own experience, that your personal dream holds a gift that is just waiting to be opened by you…the future Champion.

If you are willing to take that first step and believe in yourself and what you have already been given in the details of your personal dream, then get ready for the adventure of a lifetime! This gift will keep giving your whole life as you continue to take the steps and work at it. There will be no one who can predict exactly how your dream will happen or when, so don't worry about answering those questions when you first start out. Your success and the timing of it will be determined by you and how much you are willing to believe in yourself.

Are you willing to believe in yourself? If you said yes, I have good news for you! You have already taken your first step to achieving your dream of becoming a Champion. Now let me show you some more secrets I learned along the way to achieving my dream in the sport of Polo.

CHAPTER TWO

OWN YOUR DREAM

You will need to learn to own your dream, as you travel on the journey, because people will challenge it with lots of questions. People that don't see what you see. So be ready for them and keep believing in yourself and your dream. Never give up. Your dream is yours. The dream belongs to you. You need to know that and never think twice about it. Your dream is unique and that will sometimes be the hardest thing to deal with as a young person...the fact that you are different. There may be no one else who sees or feels what you feel and that is ok. In fact, that is the BEST part of what I am going to explain to you in this book. That is what makes you so unique and special. That is what holds the most power and you need to learn to own that power.

Your dream is a personal gift that was planted in you for a reason and it was planted in only you. Your job is to get to work and open the gift. Don't worry if your dream doesn't look like anyone else's, that's the best part. That will be what makes you so different and that is perfectly ok. In fact, that is GREAT. You need to know that your absolute best chance at becoming a true Champion is knowing you have something that no one else has and that… is your personal dream. That is also the gift you have that makes you different. That will be your extra edge over everyone else. That is what makes you unique and in order to be a Champion you need to be unique, different and stay true to yourself in the pursuit. Your individual dream is like no other gift you will ever receive in your whole life and you owe it to yourself to check it out and start opening the gift by doing the work.

My dream was completely different, completely unique. I knew what I wanted to do and I never gave up on what I saw in my unique dream. Never. I always believed, that if I did the work it would happen. In fact, my dream was so different that I never told anyone. I kept it a secret that only I knew. I never told a single person my entire personal dream, until after I achieved it.

I had the most amazing journey along the way and that is why I am writing this book. I want to share with everyone who has a dream in them, what can happen if you will just believe in yourself and your own personal dream and go to work at achieving it. Your dream will be your personal guide along the way and it is possible. My story is proof of this fact. That is how I did it and you can too.

My dream happened, because I believed in what I saw. It was mine. I was the only one who saw it and the only one who felt the power it gave me when I thought of it. That power and peace that it gave me is what fueled the mission and still fuels it today. The gift was planted in only me. It was mine to open and that is just what I did.

Your personal dream is the ticket to an adventure and journey, you don't want to miss out on. My dream took me around the world and to Polo competitions in eleven countries and gave me the opportunity to play Polo with the best players in the entire world. You need to realize your dream is yours. It is unique, just like you and that is the greatest part. Learn to own it. It is a gift made especially for you and no one else, that is just waiting to be opened by you.

CHAPTER THREE

IS YOUR DREAM REAL?

You will know your dream is real by a few clear signs. If you have already experienced what I am about to explain, then I want you to stop reading for a second and really think about your dream, after this chapter. I am here to tell you that these things happened to me. They were consistently happening to me the whole journey on my dream. Since the beginning, they were there. They are what lead me the whole way to becoming a Champion and to achieving my dream in the sport of Polo.

❖ When you think about your dream, does it light you up inside with excitement?

❖ Does each time you think about that one thought, that one dream or one goal you want to become or do, make you feel like you can't wait to go check it out or get started?

I am telling you the truth. If those two things have already happened, you have a dream inside of you just waiting to get out and it IS REAL!

Guess what? There is more good news. You already posses the magic to get your dream started. If you just answered yes to those questions, than it IS FOR REAL. You already have a real dream inside of you. A real dream holds a huge amount of power and information so get ready. It's a fact. You have one!

How do I know this? Those two things are what I started with and I not only became a Champion, but I achieved my entire dream and changed the world in the process by following those two things. I didn't mean to change the world, it just happened by what conquering my dream did for other people. It made them happy and gave them hope that dreams can come true, even the impossible and unique ones like mine

That is what becoming a Champion is all about. It starts with you and knowing if you have a real dream inside of you. That's where it all starts.

Do you already have those two things happening to you?

CHAPTER FOUR

YOU SEE IT, BUT NO ONE ELSE DOES

You see your dream, but no one else does. Has that happened to you yet? I am here to tell you, that it is ok for only you to know. In fact, for some of you, it may have to be a secret until you get farther on the journey. My dream stayed a secret that I told no one...ever. In fact, the first time I started to talk about my dream, the whole dream, was after I achieved it. What I wanted to do no woman had ever done and not in the history of the sport...ever. If I had explained what I wanted to do, for sure there would have been nobody to see or believe in what I saw because of how impossible that seemed at the time. I did so many interviews along the way with reporters who asked me all kinds of crazy questions about what I was doing along the way and challenging me with their questions, but I never gave up on what I saw. No matter how many times I was asked or challenged by people along the way to tell me I should be doing what all the other kids my age were doing, I never gave up on what I saw in my dream.

That is what dreams are all about. Doing what you see and no one else does. That's why other people think they are impossible. You are the only one who got the dream. It is your personal gift just waiting to be opened and only you got this special one.

You are the one that can make it happen. Other people did not get the gift of your dream, only you did. That is why they do not see it yet. Your next step is to be brave enough to go after it. It doesn't matter when or how long it takes and you don't need to focus or pay attention to knowing those answers when you start. That is the trick that stops most people and you don't need to fall for it. What you need to know is that the best way to achieve your personal dream is to focus on what you see. Really focus on what it is. That unique dream that only you have, focus on that. That is what you have, that no one else received. That is the special and powerful part and it holds a roadmap of information that will unfold as you go, if you will stay focused on it. No one else got your dream or roadmap. That is why they may not believe it is possible or see what you see.

Do not worry about explaining to people what they do not see, just believe in yourself and your gift and continue to do the work. Your gift was planted in you for a reason. You have to own it. It is up to you to achieve it and that is the fun part. You have to be brave enough to own your personal dream, even if no one else sees it and asks you why you are doing such an impossible thing. You have to keep working for it to happen. If you will do those things I just explained, your dream is more possible than you ever imagined. That is what happened to me and that is how I became a Champion.

If you are willing to be brave enough to own your own dream and go for it, you can become a Champion. The fact that you are unique and are the only one to have this special dream is a GREAT thing. That is the magic that no one else received…only you. There is one more thing for you to know. Get ready, because the journey to becoming a Champion will be more exciting than you ever imagined ☺!

Sunny Hale

CHAPTER FIVE

WHAT WAS MY DREAM?

My dream was to play with the best Polo players in the world, because they asked me to be there.

There was one small glitch with my dream coming true. That one small glitch made it look completely impossible. The sport of Polo is over 2,000 years old and the normal way of thinking up to that point in history, that people were used to back when I started out in my dream, was that girls could play Polo amongst other girls, but were never considered as an option for professional team mates at the top of the sport. Those professional spots were for men and young boys only is what everyone believed, because that is the way it had always been in history. The glitch which made my dream look impossible to everyone else, who did not get or see the unique dream I received, was this. I was 100% young girl who had a small personal dream. I wanted to be on one of those teams at the top and not because of some special circumstance, but because I earned the spot.

What is my sport? My sport is called Polo. The one played on horseback. The sport of Polo dates back over 2,000 years and is often referred to as the Sport of Kings. Now you see the small glitch I was dealing with? It takes four players per team and each player has a group of horses they use to compete on in the games. The field we play on is grass and about the size of nine football fields put together in size. Our horses get up to speeds of about 30-40 miles per hour and each player uses about 4- 6 horses in each game. The games last about an hour to an hour and a half to play and are played all over the world. Your horses have to be really well trained and the players have to work together as team mates passing the ball between each other, like a big game of keep away, until the team is in position to score a goal.

Women play polo and have for many generations, but when I started out in my dream, there were no women professional polo players on the top teams in the sport. All of the those professional spots were taken by men and most people did not believe women could be good enough to play at the top level of the sport. In fact, people thought it was impossible to think a woman could ever be hired to play on one of those teams. Completely impossible to imagine at the time.

I was even told not to try, many times and that women were never looked at like that and never would be. I followed my dream anyway and kept doing the work.

I wanted to be the best polo player I could be and was not trying to be anyone else. I was not trying to break anyone else's records. I was not trying to win a certain trophy or single title. I just wanted to be the best I could be so that I could get a chance to achieve my dream in the sport of Polo. I dreamed of the best players in the world asking me to play on their team, because they really wanted me to be there. Meaning they wanted me to be there more than any other person in the world. That would be like the best NFL or NBA players asking me to play on their team instead of someone that already had a spot on the team. That also meant that, they would be asking a girl to play and there were no girls on the team either. That is the way it had always been in the world. Nobody believed it could be any different at the time. I just really wanted to play with them and be a part of the team as one of them. That was my dream. I wanted the best players, those guys to ask me to play on their teams.

In the sport of Polo, all of the professional players at the top are men. All of the teams at the time when I had this dream were hiring only men or young boys. No girls ever got that spot or were even considered as a possible choice. Ever. I was a girl who wanted one of those spots on their team. I always thought that if I did the work my dream could come true. If I were good enough, then it would happen...I would get invited by the best polo players in the world to play with them. I always believed that. That was my dream. I never told anyone what I am telling you now, like this in detail. But that is what I saw in my unique dream and I truly believed it could happen. I saw that clearly and never gave up.

Well guess what? After lots and lots of hard work, I did it. I achieved my dream. I also achieved my dream exactly how I wanted to and that was with no special circumstances, but because I earned the spots on the teams in my playing abilities. That was another part of my dream that was really important to me. I wanted to earn the spot, not be given it for any special circumstance and I did it. When I say I did it, I mean for over 20 polo seasons, over and over again this invitation from the best polo players in the world kept happening. I got invited to play as a professional player with almost all of them who were considered the best in the world. The best teams at the highest level of the sport kept calling me to come play on their teams as a professional player and we won all kinds of tournaments. Sometimes I was the only girl on the field or in the entire tournament. That was the dream and honor of a lifetime to play with all of those teams and top players. That was my dream and I loved every single minute if it. What an amazing gift that is still giving today.

What an exciting ride and truly fantastic adventure. The dream only happened, because I was willing to take the first step and believe in myself and the gift that was planted in me from the beginning. Those two small things that kept happening to me, that I explained to you in the beginning, is what I kept paying attention to and giving time to. Each time I would give time and thought to them, they would give back and that would lead me to my next step on the journey to achieving my dream. The dream was real and it was so unique that I couldn't even tell anyone. It was so different from what everyone else my age was thinking about or doing, that nobody would have believed me if I told them what I saw in my dream at the time. Well guess what? I did it.

My greatest and most fun victory was the day I changed history by becoming the first woman in the world to win the US Open Polo Championships playing as a professional for the Outback Steakhouse Polo Team. The US Open Polo Championships is the most important Polo tournament in the entire United States and people travel from all over the world to compete in it. On that day, I became the first woman in the world to ever become a US Open Champion. No woman had done it in the 125-year history of the sport in the United States. Was I proud? Absolutely so proud, but there was an even bigger gift in the Championship win that day. How I got on that team is the greatest part. That was where my dream truly came true, as the best polo player in the world is the one who asked me to play. The original team they had started with for the tournament and were using in the warm up tournaments in preparation for the Open had been scrapped and when they revised the player roster is when I got the call. The best player in the world and maybe of all time, Adolfo Cambiaso is the one who told his team owner who he wanted on the team. That is the day I got the call and they could have chosen any top player in the world in any country. That is the moment the dream came true even greater than I ever imagined. That is why it is so important for you to follow your unique dreams too.

Believe in small dreams, they can come true.

That was my dream and one I am very proud of following and all that happened on the journey to achieving it. What an absolute honor to play among the best players in the world accepted as one of them. That was my dream.

CHAPTER SIX

JUST GO TO WORK

Get started on your dream and I mean today. Don't wait any longer. Today is the best day to make a decision your dream is for real and it can happen. As soon as you make that decision your life is about to change, so get ready. I can tell you that the best thing I ever did, was to truly go to work on learning all I could about what I loved to do. It was the exact right thing to do and it all came from what inspired me. That is the truth. Each step I took, each lesson I learned, each new skill I mastered and each new goal within the dream, all came from what inspired me in my own dream. That is why I can tell you with expert advice, that this works and is only waiting on you to get started.

Right now, is there something in your mind that gets you excited when you think of your dream? You can get started on it today. If you already know something that inspires you, go for it...start there. Start with that one small tiny thing, just go to work at what you feel it is telling you or calling you to go check out. Start there and see where it goes. That is how it started for me and how it was the whole way on the journey to becoming a Champion in my sport. Becoming a Champion takes true work and a lot of it. That is why a Champion is so different and special. Work is what makes Champions. They are willing to do the work it takes to learn what they don't know, until one day they can do that one thing better than anyone else in the world. If you want to be a Champion, you need to realize this fact right in the beginning. The greatest work you will ever do is the work you love. That is what becoming a Champion is all about. They love what they do and they become better than anyone else at that one thing.

To achieve my dream took a whole lot of work, but I absolutely loved what I was doing in each and every step of the way. Each skill you need to have to be a great polo player takes time to master. You have to learn how to ride a horse, really well. You have to learn to hit the ball, really well. You have to learn the strategy of the game, really well as it will be like playing a game of Chess at 35 miles an hour if you learn the right moves to make. You have to learn how to be a teammate and get a long with all kinds of players and their abilities. You have to learn how to win and not become stupid after. You have to learn how to lose and be able to find the lesson why you lost. You have to learn how to train horses and actually how to train horses better than anyone else if you want to have the best horses. You have to learn how to choose a great horse when you go to buy a new prospect. You have to learn how not to bite, when people get upset on the field and start yelling at you when the game heats up. You have to learn how to do interviews with media and not let the attention go to your head or push you in the wrong direction.

You have to learn that it is ok and actually a great thing, to stay away from the things that everyone else is doing while you are working on your dream, like drinking alcohol, partying and drugs. It takes work to be able to say no to those things and all the parties that go along with your success as it happens, but this is one of the greatest lessons every aspiring Champion needs to know and work at. These kinds of things will challenge you and they mean to steal your dream. It is the work of a Champion to learn to say no when everyone else is doing it and wants you to join them. It is a bad decision to do drugs so don't fall for it, no matter who is pushing you. Always remember this fact I will share with you now. Doing drugs will cancel your dream and Champion potential 100%. Your dream will be over the minute you say yes and get started. That one bad decision will cancel your dream forever. Work at saying no every single time someone tries to offer them to you and be proud of your goal to become a Champion. True Champions know it takes work not to fall for that trick and now you do too.

With the right attitude and work ethic you can learn more than you ever realized. The work is where you become the kind of Champion you want to be. The more work you put into it, the bigger Champion you have the chance to be. Stay on track in your dream by doing the work. Work will be your new best friend on the journey to becoming a Champion. Work at learning all of the stuff you will need to know to become the best at what you choose. It will guide you, it will give you confidence, it will give you knowledge, it will give you strength and it will give you the tools you need to become more than you ever dreamed. Do not be afraid to go to work on your dream and I suggest you get started today. And remember what I said. The hardest work you will do in the whole journey will be the work it takes to complete step #1 that I explained in Chapter One. You have to believe in your self and keep believing in yourself. That is part of the work and you need to become great at it to become a Champion.

CHAPTER SEVEN

WHAT IS A TRUE CHAMPION?

A true Champion is someone who follows their dream and doesn't let anything or anyone stand in their way. They work hard at their dream. They don't complain about coming in second, they just keep working at their dream until one day they become the Champion. A true Champion is someone who can inspire you to want to be like them without ever speaking to you. A true Champion is someone who knows how to do something better than anyone else. A true Champion is born with a dream. A Champion starts out as a young kid who had a big idea that just wouldn't go away. That big idea is called the beginning. Every Champion started with a single thought in their mind and then decided to believe in themselves and go for it.

A true Champion is respectful to their sport and their competitors. A true Champion is a sportsman to their teammates and always makes a point to thank and be respectful of all of the people who help them along the way. It's easy to win a game and beat somebody and think you know something. But that is not what it means to be a Champion. A true Champion wins because they love what they do. They mean to be the best at what they do and they work at it until there is no one in the world who can beat them. Each victory is a lesson and each loss is a lesson. They are both the same. Wins and losses hold a lot of value and a lot of information and a true Champion knows they need a lot of both of them to learn all of the lessons. A true Champion knows how to lose and they know how to win. That is what makes a true Champion different, than someone who is able to win a few times.

If your dream and goal is to become a Champion, the kind that holds the power to change the world in your sport like I did, than go to work on it and stay true to what inspires you. Your personal dream is the gift that makes you so unique and so special. Your personal gift is what holds the greatest power. That is the greatest part of a true Champion. That is the extra edge you have, that no one else was given. That is what holds the greatest potential. You have more power than you ever imagined inside that unique dream of yours. A true Champion stays true to themselves.

It is much easier for people to just give up and find a good excuse to say why their dream won't work. The true Champion knows it will take work and is not afraid to work. In fact, work will become the true Champion's best friend and guide along the way. A true Champion knows that work is where you learn to become confident and learn everything you will need to know. Without the work, you will never know how to become a Champion. Champions and work go together like peanut butter and jelly, it was meant to be.

A true Champion is someone just like you, who started out with a big dream and was brave enough to go after it. They were willing to take that first and hardest step to believe in themselves, even if their dream didn't look obvious to everyone else. The true Champion works for it anyway and never gives up.

CHAPTER EIGHT

ENJOY THE JOURNEY

When you decide to go for it, get ready for more than you ever dreamed of. Enjoy every minute of what is to come, because that is the true gift. When I started out on my dream and my own journey I had no idea I would travel around the world and see some of the most beautiful places on earth in the process. That is part of the hidden gift just waiting for you to open it. There are adventures, mysteries and a whole lot of fun things that are waiting to meet you along the way in your own dream. I know this for a fact, because it happened to me and is one of the greatest lasting gifts that keeps giving.

Becoming a Champion is a journey and a fun one. You will be in love with what you are doing and the time you will spend working at it will seem like it goes so fast. You will find and learn things you never imagined. Enjoy it all, this is a true gift that only you possess. Most people don't even try or know that they have a real dream in them and the dream is just waiting to come out and be seen by the world. They didn't know what they had in them that was so powerful. Now that you know for sure what you have and how powerful it is, don't let it go. Go after it and enjoy the journey…every minute of it.

When you make a choice to be the best you can be, you will be on your way to becoming a true Champion. True Champions are unique and were brave enough to stick to what they saw for themselves. They don't give up, they just do the work it takes to be the best they can be and overcome what they don't know.

Believe in your personal dream and get to work on it. You truly do have a real dream inside of you. Your dream is yours, no one else's, so learn to own your dream. Only you can make it come true. If becoming a Champion is what you have a dream to do then my advice is that when you finish this book, close it and get to work. Go for it. Always keep your dream in your mind and never give up, even if you have to make really small steps…take them. They will add up over time and that is the only way to become a true Champion. Work at it and keep your dream in your mind as your guide. That is where it all started for me and that is why I wanted to share with you what is possible. The greatest secret to ever know is that YOU have a gift inside of you. That gift was planted there for a reason. It is up to you to find it and bring it to life, no one else can do it for you.

Good luck and enjoy the journey to becoming a Champion ☺!

CHAPTER NINE

ABOUT THE AUTHOR

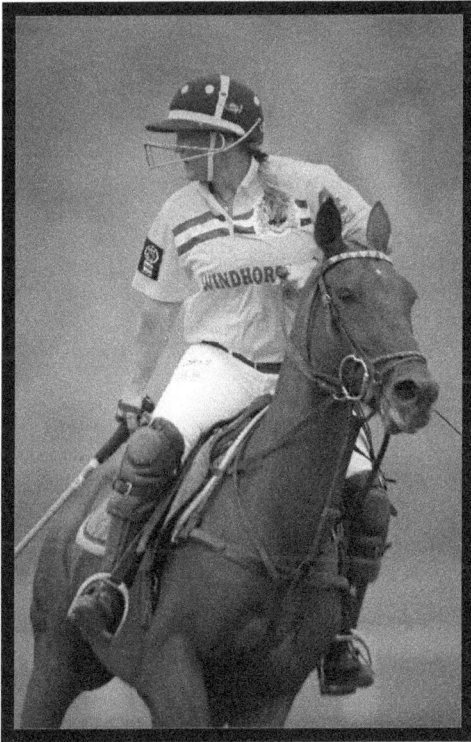

The New York Times called Sunny "the most famous female polo player in the world."

ESPNW compares her accomplishments as "Some say she's pulled off the equivalent of being the first woman to earn a World Series ring."

Sunny Hale in action / photo by Chris Yeo

Sunny Hale is widely recognized as the most accomplished and well-respected female Polo player in the world. She has competed in the Sport of Kings for over 20 years as a professional player and amassed a list of tournament titles and Championships both coed and women's tournaments like no other player in the sport's history. What sets her apart from the pack, is her achievements at the top of what has traditionally been a male dominated sport and the fact that she was hired as professional player to compete on teams alongside some of the greatest male players in the sport. Her most famous victory in Polo is the day she became the first woman in history to win the US Open Polo Championships as a professional player, hired by the world's #1 Polo Player of all time Adolfo Cambiaso and the Outback Steakhouse Polo Team. This would be the equivalent of a woman being hired to play in the NBA, World Series or the Super Bowl as a starter among the men and winning the Championships.

She has been featured in media and magazines all over the world including ESPNW, Sports Illustrated and the New York Times for her courageous and world changing accomplishments in the Sport of Kings and her true character of a Champion.

In 2012, the National Cowgirl Hall of Fame inducted Sunny, among some of the greatest American Female icons, as one of their own representing women who have changed the world. The National Cowgirl Museum and Hall of Fame honors and celebrates women, past and present, whose lives exemplify the courage, resilience, and independence that helped shape the American West. Honorees include: Sandra Day O'Connor, Georgia O'Keeffe, Annie Oakley, and Patsy Cline among other great women in American history. Sunny's story and accomplishments can now be found for all young girls to see, at the NCHF in Fort Worth Texas.

"The women who shape the West change the world".

To learn more about Sunny go to:
www.sunnyhalepolo.com

www.ingramcontent.com/pod-product-compliance
Lightning Source LLC
Chambersburg PA
CBHW031227090426
42740CB00007B/735